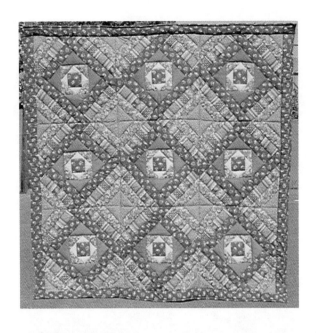

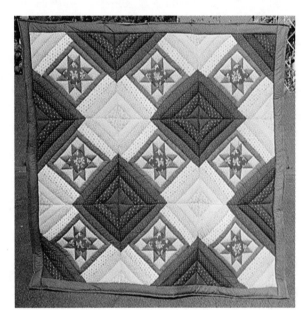

Cover Quilt

This Diamond Strip Quilt, with Borders between the Blocks, has a different Center Pattern in each block, creating a Sampler Quilt effect. The Center Patterns are all traditional patchwork patterns that are 12" in size, with a 2" finished border sewn around them. The quilt measures 96" x 96" and is owned by Karen and Jefferson Davis. Made by Rita Davis.

Quilts on the Opposite Page

Top Row

(Left) The same four fabrics have been used on all four sides of the "Square in a Square" Center Pattern in this Diamond Strip Quilt, joined without borders between the blocks. 100" x 100". Made by Rita Davis.

(Right) Log Cabin blocks of pink and brown are displayed in this quilt owned by Donna and Dave Hendrickson. 100" x 100". Made by Rita Davis.

Middle Row

(Left) Yellow and blue fabrics surround the "Square in a Square" Center Patterns in this Diamond Strip Quilt, with borders between the blocks, owned by Tracy and Mike Ingels. 96" x 96". Made by Rita Davis.

(Right) The "Evening Star" Center Pattern has been used in this Diamond Strip Quilt made by Rita Davis. 90" x 90".

Bottom Row

(Left) This Diamond Strip Quilt, joined without borders between the blocks, has "Square in a Square" Center Patterns. 100" x 100". Made by Rita Davis.

(Right) Diagonal lines of green and gold are emphasized in this Log Cabin Quilt. This arrangement of blocks is called "Straight Furrow." 100" x 100". Made by Monica Faulkner.

SIMPLE YET STUNNING QUILTS

A Step by Step Guide

Rita Davis

R.C. Publications
Portland, Oregon

R.C. Publications
   1828 N.E. Stanton
   Portland, Oregon 97212
   (503-287-1009)

Printed in the United States of America

ISBN # 0−942152−07−7

Black and White Photographs by C. Cheney
Color Photographs by Junae Hughes and Rita Davis
Publishing Coordination by Publishers Bookworks

  by Jack Sweet

Contents

Introduction		V
Chapter One:	Decisions, Decisions, Decisions	1
	Selecting a Pattern	2
	Planning Charts	2
	Shopping for Fabric	13
Chapter Two:	Sewing the Quilt Blocks	17
	Introduction	17
	The Diamond Strip Quilt	18
	Center Patterns	20
	Cutting Layout for Back Fabric and Batting	30
	Sewing the Diamond Strip Quilt Blocks	31
	The Log Cabin Quilt	41
	Center Patterns	41
	Cutting Layout for Back Fabric and Batting	44
	Sewing the Log Cabin Blocks	45
Chapter Three:	Joining the Blocks: Diamond Strip Quilts and Log Cabin Quilts	52
	Joining Blocks Without Borders between the Blocks	52
	Joining Blocks With Borders between the Blocks	58
Chapter Four:	Finishing the Quilt	62
	Outside Borders	62
	Final Outside Borders	63

TO KATHY SWEET AND MY HUSBAND, FRANK
with thanks for their love, support and enthusiasm

Introduction

Hi! I'm Rita Davis. For the past four years I have been teaching a method of machine quilting which has proven to be very successful, both with the novice sewer and the experienced seamstress. After many requests for written instructions, I have decided to write this book and take you step by step through the construction of a quilt.

And I'm talking about the construction of *beautiful* quilts. I'm talking about quilts which, although quick and easy to make, look intricate and time consuming. I'm talking about quilts which will, let's face it, impress your family and friends. So when you exclaim, "Look at the quilt I made!", you'll hear comments like these . . . "You made that? It's gorgeous! It must have taken you forever. With all you do, how do you find time to be so creative?"

Are you intrigued? Are you inspired? Then let's get started . . .

Chapter 1
Decisions, Decisions, Decisions

Which pattern should I use? What materials do I select? What colors should I make my quilt? What size should it be? How much fabric will I need?

These are all decisions which must be made before you can begin sewing. Sometimes these decisions are the hardest part of the entire project. With a little background knowledge however, they can become easier and much more enjoyable to make.

So to begin, let me give you some very basic information about quilts. Quilts are composed of three layers. The top layer of the quilt has the design on it; it may be a pieced design (patchwork) or an applique design (one fabric sewn atop another fabric). Batting comprises the middle layer of the quilt. The batting is the fluff of the quilt, and by altering the type of batting you select, you can change the thickness, the weight, and the warmth of your quilt. The bottom layer of the quilt is generally a solid or printed piece of fabric.

These three layers in a quilt must be fastened together so they do not shift around. Fastening can be accomplished by tying the quilt with thread or yarn, by hand quilting, or by machine quilting. There are two methods of machine quilting. The first technique involves piecing the entire top, and then basting the three layers together. The final step consists of running the entire quilt through the sewing machine and top stitching along the seam lines. This technique requires a lot of room, a strong back, and a high powered sewing machine. Because all of us are not equipped with these requirements, this book will focus on the second method of machine quilting.

This method, or "my method" as I typically refer to it, is also known as "block-by-block" quilting. What makes "my method" faster, and easier, than most block quilts, is that my blocks are big. My blocks range from 20" square to 36" square. Obviously, the bigger the block, the fewer you have to make, and the fewer you make, the quicker it goes.

Step One:
Selecting a Pattern

Armed with this information, you are now ready to make your first decision: selecting a pattern. This book shows the construction of two different quilts; the Diamond Strip Quilt and the Log Cabin Quilt. Each quilt can have many different looks, as you will see from the photographs.

Choose the quilt pattern you like best as the one you will make first. Please do not select one simply because it "looks easier" than another one. All quilts featured in this book are easy to make. Remember that quilts can last a lifetime — even longer with care and love — so "like the quilt you are working on" and you will find the time spent sewing it goes very quickly.

Step Two:
Planning Charts

Once you have selected a pattern, you are ready for the next step: planning the finished size of the quilt. The next few pages contain charts for each type quilt: the Diamond Strip and the Log Cabin. The charts give sample sizes of finished quilts and the yardage requirements for each.

To use the charts follow these steps:

1. **SELECT A BASIC PATTERN:** either Diamond Strip or Log Cabin. If you select Diamond Strip, decide whether or not you want borders between the blocks. (Hint: For the first Diamond Strip Quilt you make, you will probably find it easier to sew it with borders between the blocks.) It is traditional to join Log Cabin blocks without borders between them.

2. **MEASURE YOUR BED:** Measure the top of the mattress and the distance down the sides you want the quilt to hang. For example, if you have a double bed, the mattress probably measures 54" x 74". If you want to make a quilt that will be used with a dust ruffle, you might want a 12" drop. In this case you would add 12" to the sides and foot of your bed measurements. The finished size of your quilt would then be 78" x 86" (54" + 12" + 12" x 74" + 12"). For a second example, if you have a queen size bed, the mattress usually measures 60" x 80". If you want the quilt to be used as a bedspread you would measure the distance to the floor and possibly find it to be 20". In this case the finished size of your quilt would be 100" x 100" (60" + 20" + 20" x 80" + 20"). These measurements do not allow for a pillow tuck. If you want one, add an extra 10" to the length of your quilt. Sometimes however, a pillow tuck distorts the quilt pattern as it appears on the bed, so I prefer to either use pillow shams or simply to lay my quilt over the pillows without tucking it in.

3. **TURN TO THE CHART** and find the quilt which comes closest to the size you wish to make. For example, if the double bed coverlet sample for the Diamond Strip Quilt with borders between the blocks measures

84" x 89" and you would prefer 90" x 95", you have two options. You could make each block measure 25" rather than 23". Or you could increase the size of each "B" border by 1½". Either of these two methods would give you the extra 6" you want.

4. **WRITE DOWN YOUR YARDAGE REQUIREMENTS.** The charts on the following pages list the yardage required for each quilt. All yardage is based on fabric which is 45" wide and batting which is 48" wide. The only yardage not given on these pages is that for the Center Patterns. As you can see from the photographs, different Center Patterns can be used in the quilts. This book shows three different Center Patterns for each type of quilt; the Diamond Strip Quilt and the Log Cabin Quilt. After selecting the Center Pattern you will use, turn to the directions for assembling these patterns. There you will find the pattern templates and the yardage requirements listed.

Yardage Chart for Diamond Strip Quilt WITH BORDERS between the Blocks

Close up Detail of One Block in Quilt

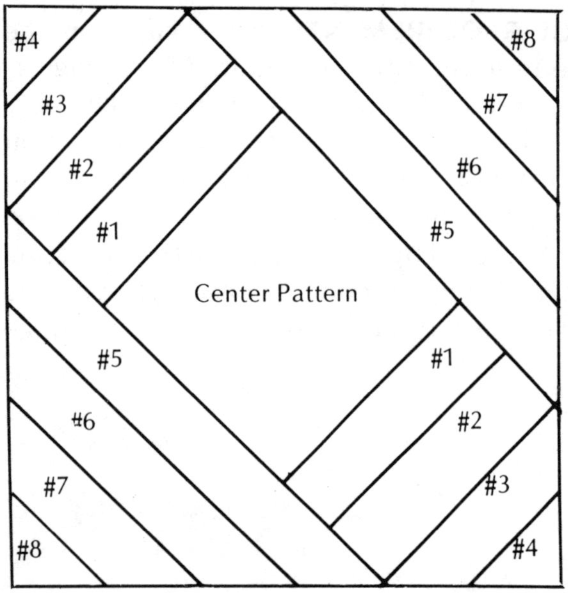

Fabrics #1, #2, #3, and #4 are usually all from the same color family (such as yellows) while Fabrics #5, #6, #7, and #8 are from another color family (such as greens). Fabrics #5, #6, #7, and #8 will be the dominant color group in your quilt.

If you want to repeat any of Fabrics #1 through #8 in your Center Pattern or borders, add yardage requirements together. For example, in the Twin Bedspread size, if you wanted Fabric #1 to also be Border A, you would purchase 1¾ yards (¾ + 1). If Fabric #5 would also be used as Border B and the Back, you would purchase 10¾ yards (1½ + 2¾ + 6½).

	Top of Quilt											Back of Quilt		Batting
Size	**Center Pattern**	**1**	**2**	**3**	**4**	**5**	**6**	**7**	**8**	**Border A**	**Border B**	**Back incl. Border B**	**Back Border A**	**Batting**
Twin Bed Coverlet	See Individual Pattern for Yardage	¾	¾	¾	½	1	¾	¾	½		2	6		6
Twin Bedspread		¾	¾	¾	½	1½	1	1	½	1	2¾	6½	1	7
Double Coverlet		1	1	1	¾	1¼	1¼	1	¾	¾	2¾	8½	¾	9
Double Bedspread		1¼	1¼	1¼	¾	2¼	1¼	1¼	¾		2¾	9		9
Queen Coverlet		1	1	1	¾	1¼	1¼	1	¾	¾	3	8½	¾	9
Queen Bedspread		1¼	1¼	1¼	¾	2¼	2¼	1¼	¾		3¼	9½		9½
King Coverlet		1¼	1¼	1¼	¾	2¼	2¼	1¼	¾		3	9½		9½
King Bedspread		1½	1½	1½	1	2½	2½	1½	1		3¾	11		11

Yardage amounts are given in yards, based on material which is 45″ wide and batting which is 48″ wide. Yardage given is enough for all blocks in the quilt. If Twin Bed Coverlet Fabric #1 shows ¾ yard, that means ¾ yard of fabric will be enough fabric for all 6 blocks in that quilt.

Diamond Strip Quilt, WITH BORDERS BETWEEN BLOCKS, Planning Chart*

TWIN BED COVERLET
58" x 85"

TWIN BEDSPREAD
75" x 92"

DOUBLE BED COVERLET
84" x 89"

DOUBLE BEDSPREAD
94" x 94"

*All measurements shown are *finished* sizes of blocks and borders.

6

Diamond Strip Quilt, WITH BORDERS BETWEEN BLOCKS, Planning Chart*

QUEEN BED COVERLET
85" x 93"

	B 4"				
	A 4"				
B 4"	23"	B 4"	23"	B 4"	23"
	B 4"				
B 4"	23"	B 4"	23"	B 4"	23"
	B 4"				
	23"	B 4"	23"	B 4"	23"
	A 4"				
	B 4"				

QUEEN BEDSPREAD
100" x 100"

	B 4"				
B 4"	28"	B 4"	28"	B 4"	28"
	B 4"				
B 4"	28"	B 4"	28"	B 4"	28"
	B 4"				
	28"	B 4"	28"	B 4"	28"
	B 4"				

KING BED COVERLET
96" x 96"

	B 4"				
	27"	B 3½	27"	B 3½	27"
	B 3½ "				
B 4"	27"	B 3½	27"	B 3½	27"
	B 3½ "				
	27"	B 3½	27"	B 3½	27"
	B 4"				

KING BEDSPREAD
112" x 114"

	B 5"				
	32"	B 4"	32"	B 4"	32"
	B 4"				
B 4"	32"	B 4"	32"	B 4"	32"
	B 4"				
	32"	B 4"	32"	B 4"	32"
	B 5"				

*All measurements shown are *finished* sizes of blocks and borders

Yardage Chart for Diamond Strip Quilt WITHOUT BORDERS Between the Blocks

Close-up Detail of one Block in Quilt

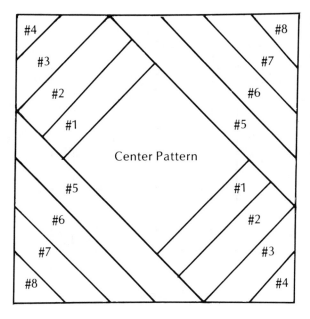

Fabrics #1, #2, #3, and #4 are usually all from the same color family (such as rusts) while Fabrics #5, #6, #7, and #8 are from another color family (such as browns). Fabrics #5, #6, #7, and #8 will be the dominant color group in your quilt.

If you want to repeat any of Fabrics #1 through #8 in your Center Pattern or borders, add yardage requirements together. For example, in the Twin Bedspread size, if you wanted Fabric #1 to also be Border A, you would purchase 2 yards (1 + 1). If Fabric #5 would also be used as Border B and the Back, you would buy 9¾ yards (1¾ + 1½ + 6½).

Size	Center Pattern	Top of Quilt										Back of Quilt		Batting
		1	2	3	4	5	6	7	8	Border A	Border B	Back incl. Border B	Back Border A	Batting
Twin Bed Coverlet		¾	¾	¾	½	1½	1	1	½		1½	6½		6
Twin Bedspread	See Individual Pattern for Yardage	1	1	1	½	1¾	1¾	1	½	1	1½	6½	1	7
Double Coverlet		1¼	1¼	1¼	¾	2	1¼	1¼	¾	¾	1½	8	¾	8¼
Double Bedspread		1¼	1¼	1¼	¾	2¼	1¼	1¼	¾	1½	1½	8½	1½	9½
Queen Coverlet		1¼	1¼	1¼	¾	2	1¼	1¼	¾	¾	1¾	8½	¾	8¾
Queen Bedspread		1¼	1¼	1¼	¾	2¼	2¼	1¼	¾	1½	1¾	10	1½	10½
King Coverlet		1½	1½	1½	1	2¼	2¼	1¼	¾		1¼	9½		9
King Bedspread		1½	1½	1½	1	2½	2½	1½	1	1½	2¼	10	1½	11

Yardage amounts are given in yards, based on material which is 45" wide and batting which is 48" wide. Yardage given is enough for all blocks in the quilt. If Twin Bed Coverlet Fabric #1 shows ¾, that means ¾ yard of fabric will be enough for all 6 blocks in that quilt.

8

Diamond Strip Quilt, WITHOUT BORDERS between Blocks, Planning Chart*

```
┌─────────────────────────┐
│    B    5"               │
│  ┌───────────┐           │
│  │ 25"  │ 25"│           │
│  ├──────┼────┤           │
│ B│ 25"  │ 25"│ B         │
│ 4"│     │    │ 4"        │
│  ├──────┼────┤           │
│  │ 25"  │ 25"│           │
│  └───────────┘           │
│    B    5"               │
└─────────────────────────┘
```

TWIN BED COVERLET
58" x 85"

```
┌───────────────────────────┐
│       B    4"              │
│   ┌──────────────┐         │
│   │ 28"  │  28"  │         │
│  B│A ├──────┼───────┤ A │B │
│  4"│5½│ 28" │  28" │5½ │4"│
│   ├──────┼───────┤         │
│   │ 28"  │  28"  │         │
│   └──────────────┘         │
│       B    4"              │
└───────────────────────────┘
```

TWIN BEDSPREAD
75" x 92"

```
┌─────────────────────────────┐
│        B    4"               │
│    ┌───────────────────┐     │
│    │     A    3"        │     │
│    │ 25" │ 25" │ 25"    │     │
│ B  ├─────┼─────┼─────┤  B     │
│ 4½ │ 25" │ 25" │ 25" │  4½    │
│    ├─────┼─────┼─────┤        │
│    │ 25" │ 25" │ 25"  │       │
│    │     A    3"        │     │
│    └───────────────────┘     │
│        B    4"               │
└─────────────────────────────┘
```

DOUBLE BED COVERLET
84" x 89"

```
┌──────────────────────────────┐
│         B  4"                 │
│    ┌───────────────────┐      │
│    │      A 4"          │      │
│    │ 26" │ 26" │ 26"    │      │
│ B │A ├─────┼─────┼─────┤ A│ B  │
│ 4"│4"│ 26" │ 26" │ 26" │4"│ 4" │
│    ├─────┼─────┼─────┤        │
│    │ 26" │ 26" │ 26"   │      │
│    │      A 4"          │      │
│    └───────────────────┘      │
│         B 4"                  │
└──────────────────────────────┘
```

DOUBLE BEDSPREAD
94" x 94"

*All measurements shown are *finished* sizes of blocks and borders.

Diamond Strip Quilt, WITHOUT BORDERS between Blocks, Planning Chart*

B 5"		
A 4"		
25"	25"	25"
25"	25"	25"
25"	25"	25"
A 4"		
B 5"		

(B 5" on left and right sides)

QUEEN BED COVERLET
85" x 93"

B 4"		
A 4"		
28"	28"	28"
28"	28"	28"
28"	28"	28"
A 4"		
B 4"		

(B 4" / A 4" on left; A 4" / B 4" on right)

QUEEN BEDSPREAD
100" x 100"

B 3"		
30"	30"	30"
30"	30"	30"
30"	30"	30"
B 3"		

(B 3" on left and right sides)

KING BED COVERLET
96" x 96"

B 5"		
A 4"		
32"	32"	32"
32"	32"	32"
32"	32"	32"
A 4"		
B 5"		

(B 4" / A 4" on left; A 4" / B 4" on right)

KING BEDSPREAD
112" x 114"

*All measurements shown are *finished* sizes of blocks and borders.

Yardage Chart for Log Cabin Quilts

Close-up Detail of One Block in Quilt

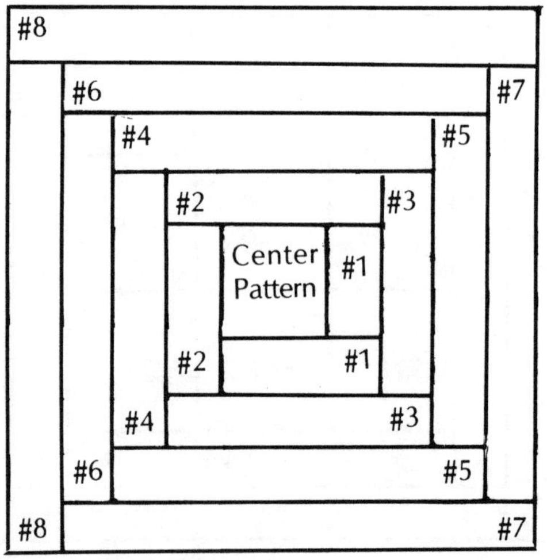

Fabrics #1, #3, #5, and #7 are usually all from the same color family (such as *dark* browns) while Fabrics #2, #4, #6, and #8 are from another color family (such as *light* tans).

If you want to repeat any of Fabrics #1 through #8 in your Borders, add yardage requirements together. For example, in the Twin Coverlet size, if you wanted Fabric #1 to also be Border A on the top and on the back of the quilt, you would purchase 3 yards (½ + 1¼ + 1¼). If Fabric #2 would also be used as Border B and the Back, you would purchase 7¼ yards (½ + 1¾ + 5).

	Top of Quilt											Back of Quilt		Batting
Size	Center Pattern	1	2	3	4	5	6	7	8	Border A	Border B	Back Incl. Border B	Back Border A	Batting
Twin Bed Coverlet		½	½	½	½	¾	¾	¾	¾	1¼	1¾	5	1¼	5¼
Twin Bedspread	See Indi-	½	½	¾	¾	1¼	1¼	1¼	1¼	1¼	1½	6¾	1¼	7
Double Coverlet	vidual Patterns	¾	¾	1	1	1¾	1¾	1¾	1¾		1½	7		6½
Double Bedspread	for Yardage	¾	¾	1	1	1¾	1¾	1¾	1¾	1¼	1¾	7¾	1¼	8
Queen Coverlet		¾	¾	1	1	1¾	1¾	1¾	1¾	¾	1¼	7½	¾	7¼
Queen Bedspread		¾	¾	1	1	1¾	1¾	1¾	1¾	1½	2	8½	1½	9
King Coverlet		¾	¾	1	1	1¾	1¾	1¾	1¾	1½	1¾	8	1½	8½
King Bedspread		1	1	1½	1½	2¼	2¼	2¼	2¼	1½	1¾	11½	1½	10½

Yardage amounts are given in yards, based on material which is 45″ wide and batting which is 48″ wide. Yardage given is enough for all blocks in the quilt. if Twin Bed Coverlet Fabric #1 shows ½, that means ½ yard of fabric will be enough fabric for all 6 blocks in that quilt.

Yardage amounts for the Back of Quilt include one yard of material which will be used to cover seams.

Log Cabin Quilt Planning Chart*

B	6"	
	A 6"	
	20"	20"
B 5" · A 4"	20"	20" · A 4" · B 5"
	20"	20"
	A 6"	
B	6"	

TWIN BED COVERLET
58" x 84"

B	3"		
	A 3"		
	20"	20"	20"
B 4½" · A 3"	20"	20"	20" · A 3" · B 4½"
	20"	20"	20"
	20"	20"	20"
	A 3"		
B	3"		

TWIN BEDSPREAD

75" x 92"

B	4½"		
	20"	20"	20" 20"
B 2"	20"	20"	20" 20" · B 2"
	20"	20"	20" 20"
	20"	20"	20" 20"
B	4½"		

DOUBLE BED COVERLET
84" x 89"

B	4"			
	A 3"			
	20"	20"	20"	20"
B 4" · A 3"	20"	20"	20"	20" · A 3" · B 4"
	20"	20"	20"	20"
	20"	20"	20"	20"
	A 3"			
B	4"			

DOUBLE BEDSPREAD
94" x 94"

*All measurements shown are *finished* sizes of blocks and borders.

Log Cabin Quilt Planning Chart*

B 3″			
A 3″			
20″	20″	20″	20″
20″	20″	20″	20″
20″	20″	20″	20″
20″	20″	20″	20″
A 3″			
B 3″			

(with B 3″ and B 3″ side borders)

QUEEN BED COVERLET
86″ x 92″

B 5″			
A 5″			
20″	20″	20″	20″
20″	20″	20″	20″
20″	20″	20″	20″
20″	20″	20″	20″
A 5″			
B 5″			

(with B 5″, A 5″ side borders left and A 5″, B 5″ right)

QUEEN BEDSPREAD
100″ x 100″

B 4″			
A 4″			
20″	20″	20″	20″
20″	20″	20″	20″
20″	20″	20″	20″
20″	20″	20″	20″
A 4″			
B 4″			

(with B 4″, A 4″ side borders left and A 4″, B 4″ right)

KING BED COVERLET
96″ x 96″

B 4″				
A 3″				
20″	20″	20″	20″	20″
20″	20″	20″	20″	20″
20″	20″	20″	20″	20″
20″	20″	20″	20″	20″
20″	20″	20″	20″	20″
A 3″				
B 4″				

(with B 3″, A 3″ side borders left and A 3″, B 3″ right)

KING BEDSPREAD
112″ x 114″

*All measurements shown are *finished* sizes of blocks and borders.

Step Three:
Shopping for Fabric

You are now ready to step on down to the fabric store and choose materials for your quilt. Selecting the fabric can really be an enjoyable experience. It can also be an incredibly time-consuming experience, and sometimes, perhaps, an overwhelming one; so let me answer some of your questions and point you in the right direction.

Where Should I Shop?

Nowadays you can buy fabric almost anywhere. Quilt stores and fabric stores are springing up in every neighborhood. Department stores, dime stores, and discount stores often carry fabric. Sometimes even grocery stores sell fabric! Each of these outlets offers something, be it price, convenience, choice, quality, or service.

Although its prices may sometimes be slightly higher, the place which offers the most advantages, particularly to the novice sewer, is the quilt store. Quilt stores usually carry only high-quality material. They only stock materials which work well in quilts, hence you are not distracted by stretchy knits or other kinds of inappropriate fabrics. Quite often they arrange all their fabrics by color, and this can help you focus quickly on the fabrics you want. And last but most important, these shops are usually staffed by experienced quilters, and their help can be invaluable.

What Types of Fabrics Should I Choose?

100% cottons and cotton blends are always good choices for quilts. Any fabric which has a fairly sturdy texture will work well in these quilts. Perhaps it would be easier to tell you what fabrics to avoid. Stay away from stretchy, knit materials. Avoid very sheer materials, or fabrics which tend to fray. Do not use a material with a very loose weave. For your early quilts, I would also suggest you back off from using velvets or silks, as they are hard to handle. It is permissible to use eyelet material, in fact, I think a small amount of eyelet can really add a touch of elegance to your quilt. Remember however, you must line eyelet with another fabric or else you may find batting peeping up through the eyelet holes.

What Colors Should I Use?

Sometimes it's hard to know where to start when you are deciding on colors for your quilt. Ask yourself this first: is there something in the room you are trying to match — for instance, the rug or the wallpaper? In this case you have one color already, and you will be looking for another color to complement it. Or are you the lucky person who is starting from scratch, one who is able to plan the room around the quilt? Then my best advice is to go down to the quilt store and pick out your favorite print fabric in the whole store.

Now look at this print closely. See what other colors have been used in the print. Is it mostly brown, with a touch of rust, blue, and white? Or is it a navy blue, with light blue and red in it? If the print appeals to you, you can feel safe using its main color as your predominant one, and selecting one of the other colors in it as your secondary color. You should realize that fabric manufacturers have on their staff artistic people who are experienced in putting colors together. These employees are educated in color-coordination, so why not take advantage of their expertise. If they have put navy and rust together in a fabric, and you like it, you can be assured that you will be pleased with a navy and rust quilt.

Should I Choose Different Fabrics for the Top Side and the Back Side of my Quilt? What about Borders?

Certain fabrics will work better on the different sides of the quilt. Let's talk about the top side of the quilt first.

My philosophy is this: "Be easy on yourself." Don't choose anything which will create problems. I've found, through experience, that the following choices of fabrics will give the best results on top of the quilt: Calicos or other small prints, Ginghams, Solids, Stripes (assuming you use them across the stripe rather than down it), and Eyelet (should be used sparingly and must be lined).

Problems sometimes develop from using the following types of fabrics on the front side of the quilt: Patchwork Prints (too busy), Directional Prints (too hard to keep track of which way they are going), Stripes (if used down the fabric rather than across they are too hard to match), and Large Prints (total effect may be missing when used in small pieces).

On the backs of quilts ladies have traditionally used muslin. Muslin was inexpensive, readily available and easy to hand quilt. Muslin is still readily available, but it's no longer that inexpensive, and with this type of quilt we will not have to worry about hand quilting it. Therefore, I prefer to use a print of some kind on the backs of my quilts.

This makes my quilts reversible. If I want a change in my bedroom, I simply flip the quilt over. Reversible quilts also stay cleaner longer. Washing quilts is quite a chore, so if you can put it off for awhile, so much the better.

The main point you want to remember when choosing material for the back of your quilt is this: you never want to worry about what's happening on the back side of your quilt when you are working on the top. I've found that Patchwork Prints or Calicos or other small prints give the best results on the backs of quilts. You will have problems if you choose any of the following fabrics for the back of your quilt: Directional Prints (you will be turning the squares in different directions to get your pattern on the front side of the quilt, and you don't want to have to worry about which way the prints on the back are matching), Stripes (too directional), Ginghams (can look directional), Solids (overemphasize machine stitching, tend to pick up dust and dirt easily), Eyelets and Sheers (too fragile).

Border fabrics can either be a repeat of one of the fabrics in your quilt block, or an entirely new fabric. Either choice can be effective. Quite often I wait until I have made all the blocks before picking out the border. This way I can really see the effect of the print I have selected. Calicos or small prints are the best choices for border fabrics. Try to avoid the following fabrics for borders: Stripes (too directional, hard to match), Ginghams (too directional, can look like they are sewn on crooked, even when not), Solids (can look puckery when used in borders), Patchwork Prints (too busy), Large Prints (design can get lost), and Eyelet (too fragile).

What Other Supplies Will I Need?

1. **BATTING:** Batting comes in various sizes: 3 oz., 5 oz., 6 oz., 7.5 oz., 8 oz., 9 oz., or 12 oz. The higher the number, the higher the loft to the batting and the more weight and warmth to the quilt. I would suggest that you use 5 to 8 oz. batting. 3 oz. batting is especially designed for hand quilters and has very little loft. Since our stitches will be further apart than a hand quilters, you'll find greater loft gives a nicer effect to machine quilts. Any batting 9 oz. or more is generally considered upholstery batting, and it is just too heavy to use. One lady I know used 9 oz. batting in a kingsize bedspread and the quilt weighed almost twenty pounds!

I've used 7.5 oz. batting in most of my quilts and have been very pleased with the results. I like the feeling of weight and warmth on cold winter nights. For my summer quilts, however, I've used 5 oz. batting. My sewing machine has no trouble sewing through either size batting. So choose whichever size you prefer. Remember that 5 oz. will give a lighter, flatter quilt, and 7.5 oz. will give a heavier, loftier quilt.

2. **THREAD:** You do not need quilting thread. In fact, quilting thread is often too thick to be threaded into the sewing machine's needle. So choose ordinary thread. I use 100% cotton thread as I have found it to be less troublesome (does not break, split or fray), but you may use a polyester blend if you prefer. You will need approximately 1,200 yards to complete your quilt. Choose a color of thread which will blend into the fabric selected for the back of your quilt. You may have been taught to always use thread that is the same color as the lightest piece of fabric with which you are sewing. Forget that! In this case, you want a thread which will "disappear" on the back side of your quilt. Whatever the predominant color of the back fabric is, choose the same color thread. If you have a navy blue background with red flowers on it, select navy thread. If you have brown fabric with white polka dots, use brown thread. If it is white fabric with brown polka dots, use white thread.

3. **PINS AND NEEDLES:** I use corsage pins when sewing these quilts. These pins are 2″ long, and have big, gaudy heads. Corsage pins have several advantages over ordinary pins. They will not get "lost" in your quilt. They are long enough to go in and out of heavy batting, and the big heads keep them from slipping into the batting forever. Their gaudy heads also make them easily recognizable when they fall on the floor or carpet. This way you'll be able to find them and pick them up before your husband, child or dog manages to step on one. You will only need about 25 of these pins to sew your quilt. If your fabric store does not carry them, try a local florist shop.

You will need one needle for hand sewing and a package of machine needles. You may use any size needle you prefer for the hand sewing. Your machine needles can be any size between 11 and 14. You might prefer size 11 if your fabrics are delicate, otherwise size 14 would be your best bet.

4. **SEWING MACHINE:** Any ordinary sewing machine will do. It does not have to be a fancy model. If it sews a straight stitch, goes forward and back, you are set to go. I personally sew on a ten-year-old Kenmore, and I'm very satisfied with it. I've had students sew on 30-year-old Singers and brand new top-of-the-line Vikings. I think I've seen almost every type of machine in my classes, and not one machine yet has refused to handle the bulk of these quilts.

5. **IRON AND IRONING BOARD:** Ironing your fabric will make it easier to sew, make your patchwork designs fit better and make a better looking quilt. If a fabric goes into a quilt ironed, it will forever look ironed. If it goes in wrinkled, it will always look wrinkled. So, I'm old fashioned. I'm going to insist you iron as you go. You'll also be using your ironing board to prop up the quilt when we get to the part about joining blocks together, and this will help you deal with the size and the weight of the quilt.

Chapter 2
Sewing the Quilt Blocks

Introduction

The hard part is over. The decisions have been made and the fabric purchased. Take the fabric home and wash it in your washing machine. Use soap and run it full cycle. I use warm water and cold rinse. Some burgundy, rust, and navy fabrics will run considerably. If you notice colored rinse water, you can add vinegar to the rinse cycle, and this should set the fabric. Then put the fabric into your dryer. This preshrinking and setting of material is a necessary step. Do not, however, under any circumstances, wash or dry your batting. Until it has been sewn into a quilt, it cannot be washed.

Set up your sewing machine in a room so that it is conveniently arranged. I work in an inverted "U" area. My machine sits in the middle; on my right side is my ironing board, and on my left is a table holding my fabrics. The more time you can eliminate from jumping up and down to fetch fabrics, the better.

You are now ready to begin sewing the blocks of your quilt. This part is divided into two sections: the Diamond Strip Quilt and the Log Cabin Quilt, so turn to the pattern you have selected.

Diamond Strip Quilt

Step One:
Making the Center Pattern

Choose a patchwork pattern you like. Three simple, effective ones are given on the next pages, but you may use any pattern you prefer as long as the size of the block is 12" (finished) and you put a 2" (finished) border around the block.

Transfer the pattern pieces (templates) onto heavy tagboard or acetate. You will notice that the patterns I have given you have a ¼" seam allowance. The edge of the presser foot on most sewing machines is ¼" away from the needle. Measure yours. If your measurement is ¼", then you can use your presser foot as a seam guide while sewing. Line up your fabric so that it is even with the presser foot and you will automatically take a ¼" seam allowance.

Place the templates on fabric that has been folded in half. This way you are cutting through two layers of fabric at once. It is best to fold the fabric so that the right sides of the fabric are together. Be sure, if you are using triangles, that you place the triangles on the fabric so that they resemble a right angle rather than a pyramid (see diagram). Triangles placed incorrectly will result in stretchy patchwork pieces which do not fit together well.

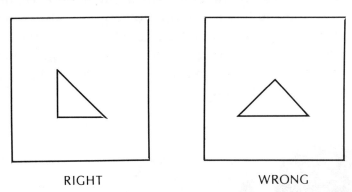

RIGHT   WRONG

Trace around the templates with a pencil. Do not use a pen or ink marker to trace around the templates as they may later run in the washing machine. If you are working on dark fabrics, and cannot see pencil markings, use chalk or soap, or try the special marking pencils sold in quilt shops to draw your lines. Place the templates right next to each other as shown in the photographs on the next page. This will save fabric as well as time spent drawing and cutting.

Sew the patchwork pieces together following the directions shown on each pattern. Be sure to iron after each step. It is better to press seams to one side rather than pressing them open. Pressing seams to one side makes the patchwork stronger, and makes it easier to match the seams.

I find it easiest to sew all of my Center Patterns at one time. If I have 9 blocks in my quilt, and I'm using "Evening Star" as the center pattern, I sew 9 "Evening Star" patterns at this step before moving on to Step 2.

Tracing the Templates onto Fabric

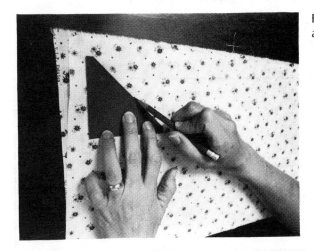

Fold the fabric in half. With pencil, trace around the first template.

Lay the template right next to the first triangle you have drawn.

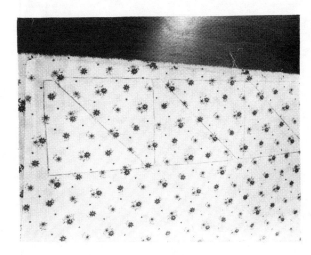

Draw remaining triangles needed in row across fabric.

Center Pattern #1:

Square in a Square Yardage Chart and Templates
This is the easiest of the three patterns.

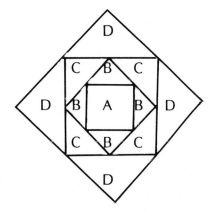

Yardage Requirements	6 Blocks	9 Blocks
A	¼	½
B	⅓	½
C	½	¾
D	1	1½

Square in a Square

"A"

Cut 1 for each Block

Center Pattern #1:
Square in a Square Templates

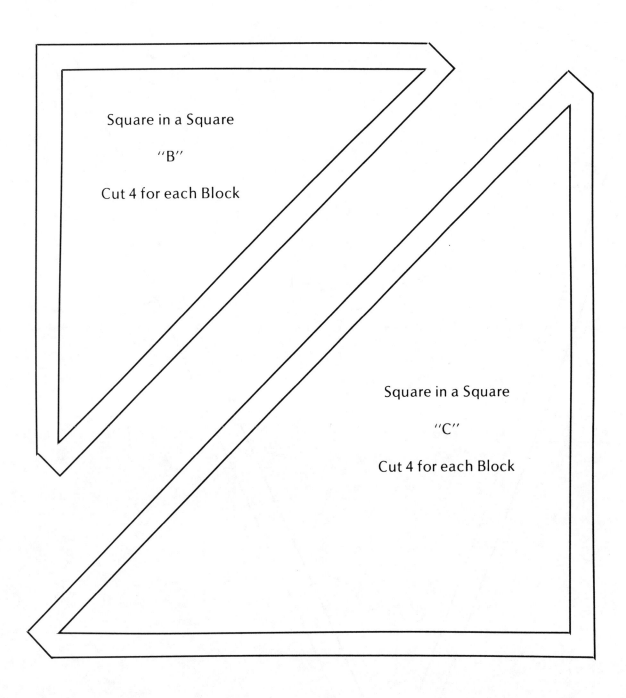

Square in a Square

"B"

Cut 4 for each Block

Square in a Square

"C"

Cut 4 for each Block

Center Pattern #1:

Square in a Square Templates

Square in a Square

''D''

Cut 4 for each Block

Center Pattern #1:

Square in a Square: Directions for Assembly

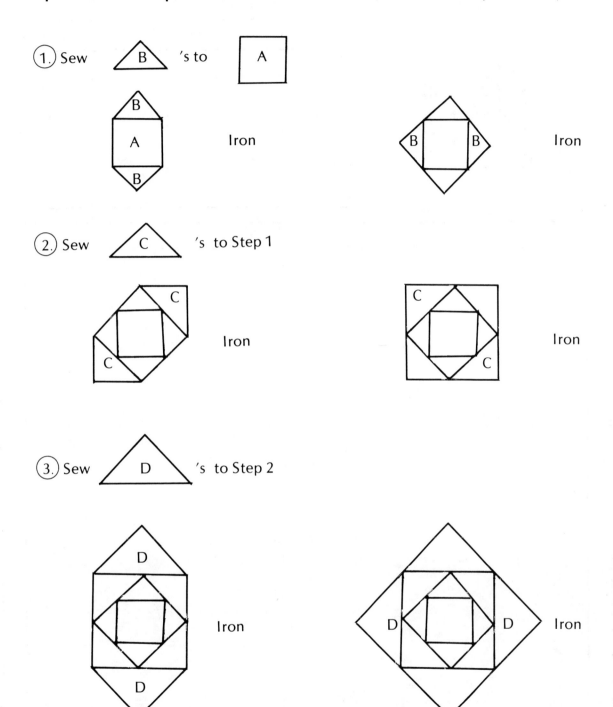

Center Pattern #2:

Evening Star Yardage Chart and Templates

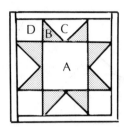

Yardage	Requirements		6 Blocks	9 Blocks
A			¼	½
B			½	¾
C	and	D	1	1 ½
Border			¾	1

Evening Star

"A"

Cut 1 for each Block

Center Pattern #2:

Evening Star Templates

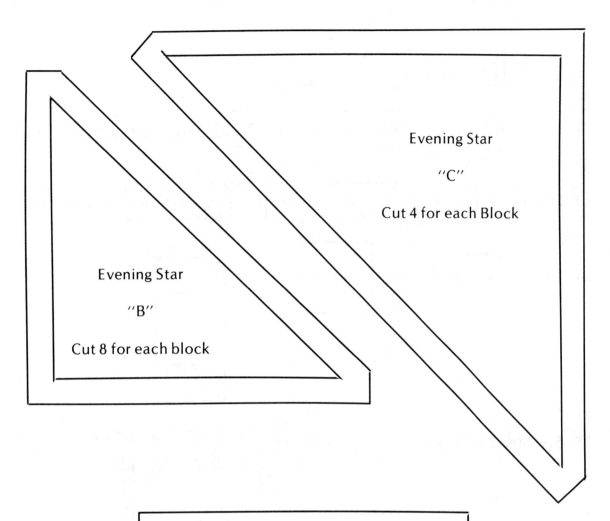

Evening Star

"C"

Cut 4 for each Block

Evening Star

"B"

Cut 8 for each block

Evening Star

"D"

Cut 4 for each Block

26

Center Pattern #2:

Evening Star : Directions for Assembly
(Remember to iron after every step)

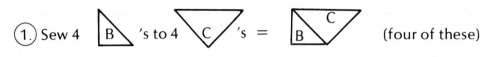

1. Sew 4 B 's to 4 C 's = (four of these)

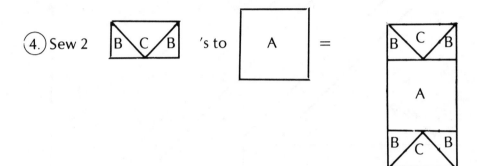

2. Sew 4 B 's to 4 B C 's = (four of these)

3. Sew 4 D 's to 2 B C B 's = D B C B D (two of these)

4. Sew 2 B C B 's to A =

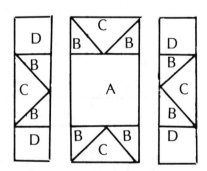

5. Sew Step 3 to Step 4

6. Sew 2½ " border around Block (will be 2" finished)

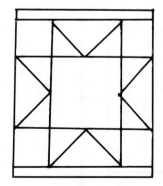

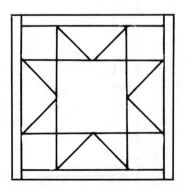

Center Pattern #3:
Weathervane Yardage Chart and Templates

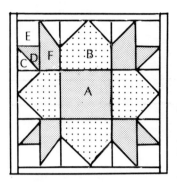

Yardage	Requirements		6 Blocks	9 Blocks
A			¼	¼
B			½	¾
C	and	E	¾	1
D	and	F	1	1¼
Border			¾	1

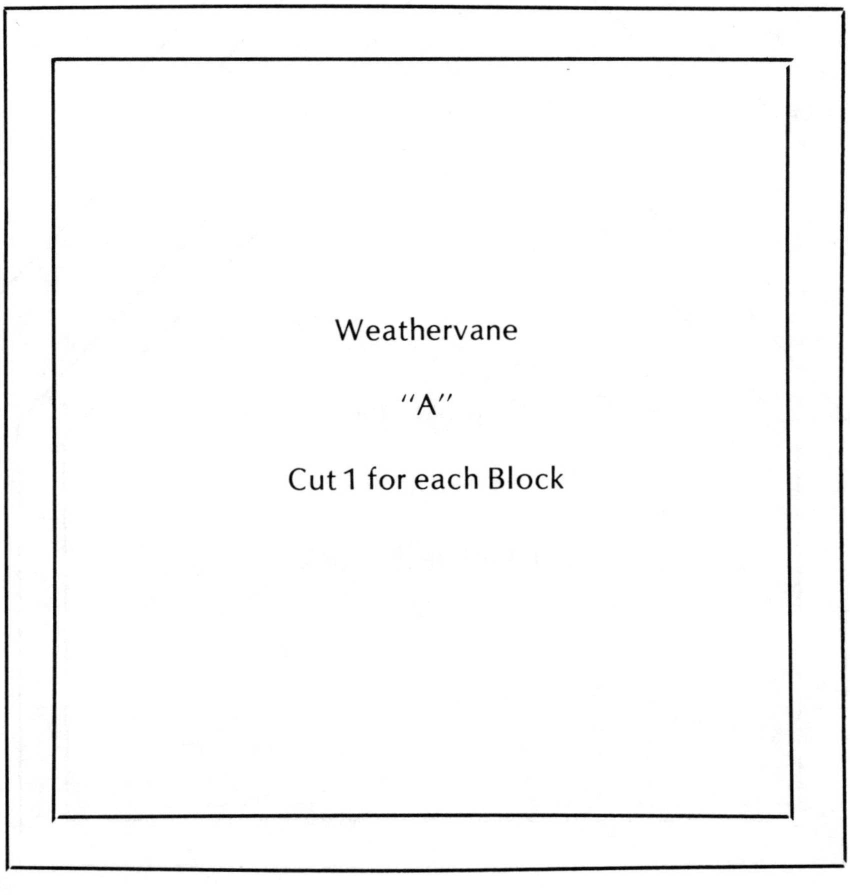

Weathervane

"A"

Cut 1 for each Block

Center Pattern #3:
Weathervane Templates

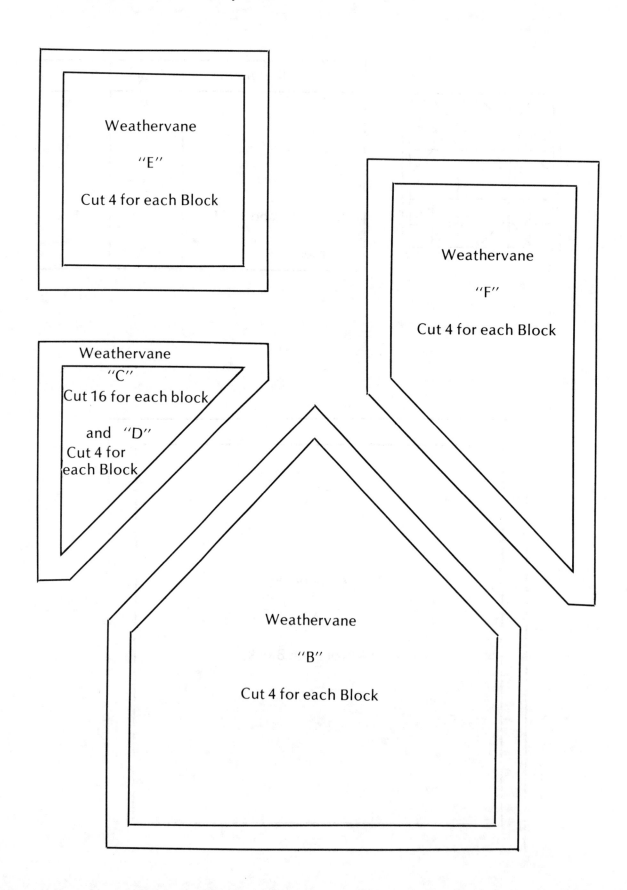

Weathervane

"E"

Cut 4 for each Block

Weathervane

"F"

Cut 4 for each Block

Weathervane

"C"
Cut 16 for each block

and "D"
Cut 4 for
each Block

Weathervane

"B"

Cut 4 for each Block

Center Pattern #3:

Weathervane : Directions for Assembly

(Remember to iron after every step)

 1. Sew D 's to C 's = DC (four of these)

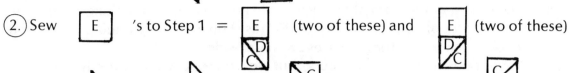 2. Sew E 's to Step 1 = E (two of these) and E (two of these)

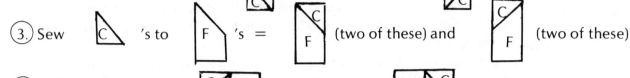 3. Sew C 's to F 's = (two of these) and (two of these)

 4. Sew Step 2 to Step 3 = (two of these) and (two of these)

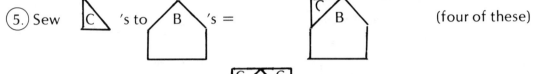 5. Sew C 's to B 's = (four of these)

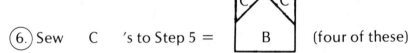 6. Sew C 's to Step 5 = (four of these)

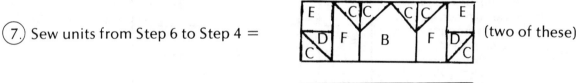 7. Sew units from Step 6 to Step 4 = (two of these)

 8. Sew units from Step 6 to A

9. Sew Steps 7 to Step 8

10. Sew 2½ " border around Block (will be 2" finished)

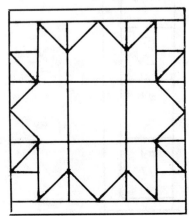
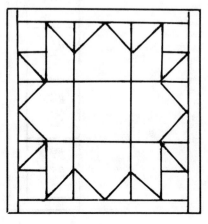

Step Two:

Cutting Layout for Back Fabric and Batting

Cut out a square of backing from the material you chose for the back of your quilt and cut a square of the same size from your batting. **The back and batting squares will be 2″ larger than the finished size square with which you will end.** This extra 2″ allows for seam allowances and shrinkage due to quilting. Therefore, if the finished size of your block is to be 25″ (as shown on the planning chart), you will cut your back and batting squares 27″ on all sides.

I have used the word "cut" here, but you may rip your fabric if you wish. Personally, I prefer to rip as I've found it is faster, and it gives a more accurate and consistent size.

The best way to cut your batting is as follows: First cut out your squares from the back material. Lay one of the squares of material on top of the batting and use it as a pattern piece to cut your batting. Batting stretches, so it does not work well if you try to measure it with a yardstick.

Use the following diagrams as a cutting guide:

EXAMPLE:
If you have 9 blocks in your quilt, and the finished size of each block is 25″, you would cut 9 blocks that are 27″ square to start. The material and batting to the right of the squares will not be wasted. It will be used later on for borders around the quilt. Be sure you do not cut across this leftover fabric then, but leave it in a nice long strip so it is usable later.

Fabric
44-45″

| #1 27″ |
| #2 27″ |
| #3 27″ |
| #4 27″ |
| #5 27″ |
| #6 27″ |
| #7 27″ |
| #8 27″ |
| #9 27″ |

Batting
48″

| #1 27″ |
| #2 27″ |
| #3 27″ |
| #4 27″ |
| #5 27″ |
| #6 27″ |
| #7 27″ |
| #8 27″ |
| #9 27″ |

Step Three:
Sewing the Diamond Strip Quilt Blocks

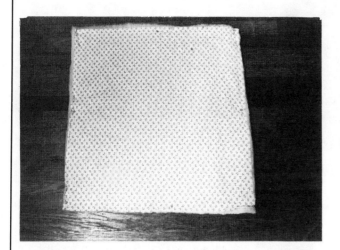

Lay one square of batting on the floor or on a table. Place one square of back fabric on the top of the batt. The right side of the fabric should be facing you. Place pins in the four corners and in the middle of each length as shown.

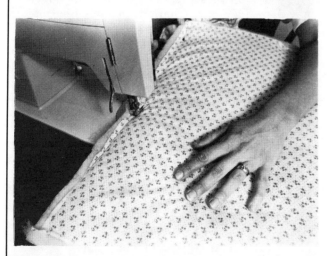

With your machine set on the longest stitch it has, baste the two layers of back and batt together. Use a ¼" seam. If the batting should somehow be a little small, just stretch it until it is the same size as the back block.

Your back and batt basted together should look like this. Do not be alarmed if it looks somewhat lumpy. These will be smoothed out as the block is quilted.

Turn the block over so that the batting is facing you. Lay your Center Pattern on the square. **Be sure to lay it so that it resembles a diamond placed on a square.** It is important to center the Center Pattern exactly. With a ruler, measure the distance from the edge of the block to the **basting** stitch you have just put in. This measurement should be the same on all four sides (or within a ½" variance at most). When properly centered, **lightly** pin the pattern to the block.

Now you must determine what size your strips will be (Fabrics #1 through #8.) **Measure the distance from the edge of the pattern to the corner of the block as shown.** This measurement should be the same on all four sides (a 1" variance is okay; any more than 1" probably means you have not centered the pattern properly). **Divide the measurement by 4** (the number of strips you will have on each side). This will be the finished size of each strip. **To this measurement, add your seam allowance.** If you are using 5 oz. batting or less, add ½". If you are using 6 oz. or more, add ¾". For example, if your measurement turns out to be 12" from corner to pattern, divide 12 by 4 and get 3. Each strip will be 3" finished. But to this 3", you must add seam allowance. If you are using 7.5 oz. batting, you would add ¾". Thus you would cut each strip 3¾". (To give myself some insurance, and room for error, I usually cut the corner strips an inch larger. Therefore, fabrics 1, 2, 3, 5, 6, and 7 would be cut 3¾" and fabrics 4 and 8 would be cut 4¾".)

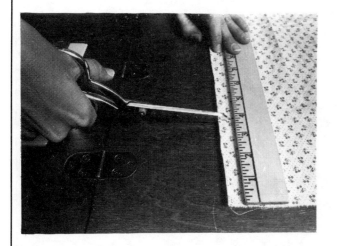

Cut or rip your strips. I prefer to rip as it is faster and usually straighter. If you bought the fabric from a store which cut it (rather than ripped it), cut a 1" notch in your fabric and rip this strip off. This will be wasted fabric but will assure you of a straight edge from which to measure. Now take your strip measurement and cut a notch at the correct place (as shown) and rip the fabric along its entire length. It does not matter if you rip across or down the fabric, although certain fabrics may rip one direction easier than another. It is usually the most economical use of fabric to rip along the longest length.

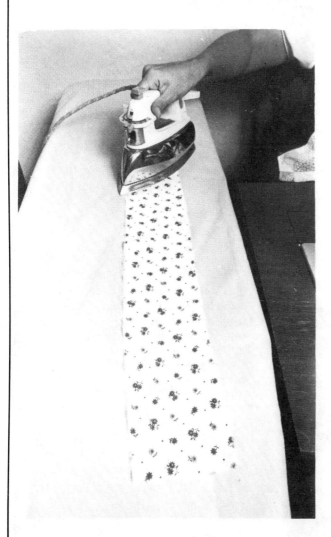

The strips you have just ripped are probably curled up at the edges and may be somewhat wrinkled. Iron them now. It is impossible to take an accurate ¼" seam allowance if edges are curling up. Remember, all strips that are sewn into a quilt ironed, generally stay looking ironed. Strips that are sewn into the quilt wrinkled seem to look that way forever. Notice that my ironing board is placed right next to my machine. I've adjusted its height to the same height as my sewing machine table. I do not have to move or even stand up to iron, thus I don't mind doing it. Try to set up your ironing board in a similar position.

Lay a strip of Fabric #1 atop one side of your Center Pattern, right sides together. Start the strip at the same point the Center Pattern begins. Do not worry if the strip is a lot longer than the Center Pattern. It should be. Do not cut it shorter, but leave it as it is. Turn your stitch length knob on your machine so that it is at 10 stitches per inch. (Most machines will easily handle this. If your machine seems to sew sluggishly, or if the stitches look too small, adjust the length to 6 or 8 stitches per inch.)

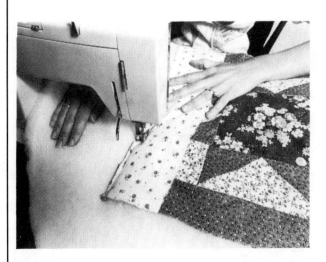

Stitch the strip to the Center Pattern using a ¼" seam allowance. Backstitch or stitch in place lightly at the start of the strip. Stitch only until you come to the end of the Center Pattern. Backstitch one or two stitches and cut your top and bottom threads. Be sure to backstitch sparingly — it is best to stitch in place if your machine has that option since everything you do on the front shows on the back. Also, be sure when you cut your bottom thread that you do not cut into the back fabric.

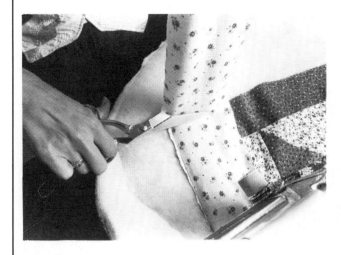

Lift up the remaining length of strip (as shown) and cut it off even with the Center Pattern.

Flip Strip #1 over so that its right side is facing you. Check the seam on the back side of the block for tucks. Hopefully, and most likely, there will be no tucks or folds in the fabric, but if there are, now is the time to find them. If you see a tuck, try to work it out with your fingers. If this is not possible, you will have to rip out some stitches, smooth the area over, and resew the seam. If you find that you are consistently having trouble with tucks, check these points: Is your stitch length too small? (Lower it to 6 or 8 stitches per inch.) Are you using a portable sewing machine? Is the arm plate on? (It should be — you need a level surface to sew on.) Does your machine sit about 3" above the table? (Try creating a level surface for the block to rest on while you are working on it. Use books or magazines to build up the area around your machine.) Is part of your block hanging off the table while you are sewing on another part of it? (This pull can distort your block and lead to tucks. Set up another table or move your ironing board to the left side of your machine, so that the block can rest on it while you sew.)

Now take a strip of Fabric #2 and place it atop Fabric #1, right sides together. Stitch the strips together, using a ¼" seam allowance, as you did in the previous step. Stitch to the end of Strip #1, lift the remaining length of Strip #2, and cut it off even with Strip #1. Flip Strip #2 over so the right side is facing you and check the back for tucks.

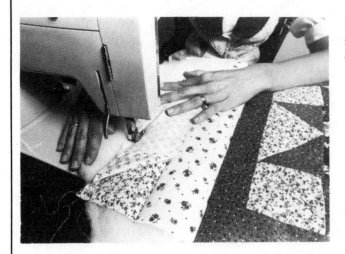

Follow the same steps for Strip #3: sew, cut off excess of strip, flip over and check for tucks.

Sew Strip #4 to Strip #3. Flip over, check for tucks and cut. This time when you are cutting off the excess material, cut Strip #4 even with the edge of the batting. Put a tacking stitch (one or two stitches on the machine) in the corner of Strip #4 to hold it in place.

Your first side is now done. Your block should look like this.

Repeat the **same steps** as above with the **same fabrics** on the opposite side of the block. To be economical with fabric, use the excess amounts of Strips 1, 2, 3, and 4 that you cut off of the first side. Your block should look like this at the conclusion of this step.

Take a strip of Fabric #5 and lay it along one of the remaining sides of the block, right side facing down. Begin Strip #5 where the batting begins and stitch to where it ends.

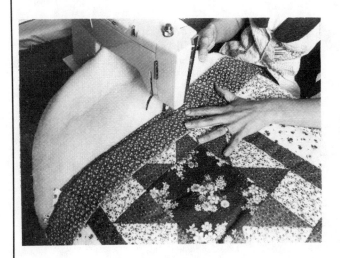

Occasionally you will have problems with tucks on the back side of your quilt when stitching Strip #5. This is because you are crossing seam lines. To avoid tucks, I keep my right hand underneath the block, and pull it slightly towards myself. This keeps the fabric on the back taut and free from folds. With my left hand on top, I try to press Strip #5 to the fabrics beneath it so the needle has a flat surface to sew over.

Flip Strip #5 over. Check for tucks. Cut your threads. Cut Strip #5 even with the batting.

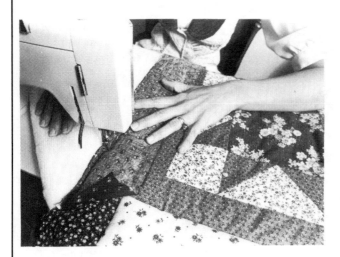

Place Strip #6 atop Strip #5, right sides together. Begin Strip #6 where the batting begins. Stitch to the end of the batting. Flip Strip #6 over and check for tucks on the back of the block. Cut your threads and cut Strip #6 even with the batting.

Sew Strip #7 to Strip #6 in the same manner. Flip over, check for tucks, and cut threads. Cut Strip #7 even with the batting.

Sew Strip #8 to Strip #7. Flip it, check for tucks, and cut threads. Cut Strip #8 even with the batting. Sew a tacking stitch in the corner.

Your third side is now done. Your block should look like this.

Repeat the **same steps** with the **same fabrics** on the remaining side of the block.

Wait up! You're not done yet. The final step consists of outlining the seams in your Center Pattern. Top-stitch (stitch in the seam lines) along any seam in the Center Pattern you wish to emphasize. You may use a straight stitch set at about 8 stitches per inch, or you may use a fancy stitch if your machine has them. Try a running zigzag or any other stitch you like.

Sew all the other blocks in your quilt in the same fashion. I've found the following preparations make the sewing go faster. I sew all my Center Patterns first. Then I sew all my back fabrics to my batting blocks at one time. I tear all my strips and hang each different fabric on a separate wire clothes hanger. (This way I can take each one off as I need it, and when I'm done sewing for the day, I can put the hangers in the closet and my sewing room looks clean.) Some people prefer to sew all of Fabrics 1, 2, 3, and 4 to each block and then move on to Fabrics 5, 6, 7, and 8. This is the fastest way. Personally, I prefer to complete one block at a time in the manner I have shown. I like the sense of satisfaction I get from completing each block, and I enjoy watching the quilt grow as each block is finished. Either method works fine, however, so choose the one you prefer.

When you have finished all your blocks, turn to Chapter 3 for directions to join them.

The Log Cabin Quilt

Step One:
Making the Center Pattern

Choose any one of the three Center Patterns for the center of your Log Cabin blocks. Read the directions on "Making the Center Pattern" for the Diamond Strip Quilt before cutting or sewing your pattern pieces together.

Center Pattern #1

This is the easiest of the three patterns. Cut one 4½" square for each block in your quilt.

Yardage Requirements	
# of Blocks in Quilt	Yardage
6	¼ yd.
12	½ yd.
16	½ yd.
25	¾ yd.

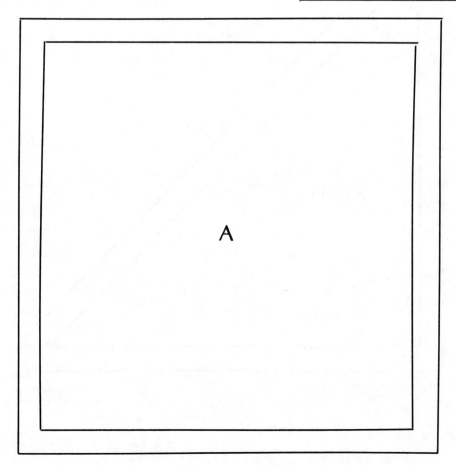

A

Center Pattern #2

This Center Pattern consists of two triangles sewn on the diagonal to make a square. Usually one triangle will be from the light color group and the other triangle from the dark color group.

Cut one triangle from each color group for each block in your quilt. Sew one dark and one light triangle together for each block.

Yardage Requirements		
# of Blocks in Quilt	A	B
6	¼	¼
12	¼	¼
16	¼	¼
25	½	½

A and B

Center Pattern #3

This Center Pattern is actually a miniature Log Cabin pattern. Pattern piece A is cut from one color group (i.e. dark) and pattern pieces B and C are cut from the other color group (i.e. light).

Sew A and B together, then join C to them.

Yardage Requirements			
# of Blocks in Quilt	A	B	C
6	¼	¼	¼
12	¼	¼	¼
16	¼	¼	¼
25	¼	¼	½

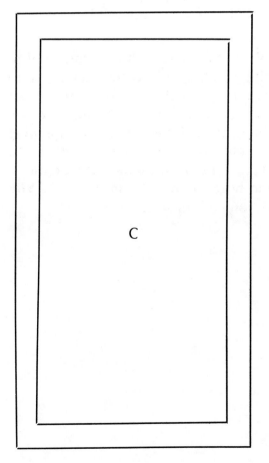

C

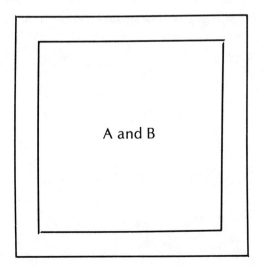

A and B

Step Two:

Cutting Layout for Back Fabric and Batting

All of the Log Cabin quilts are based on a 20" finished square. I've chosen this size since it proves to be the most economical use of fabric.

Your first step is to cut squares of back material that are 2" larger than your finished size. Thus, if you are working with the finished size of 20", you will cut out squares measuring 22" on all sides. Since material is 44/45" wide, you can get two squares across out of a piece of material 22" long.

The following diagrams show cutting layouts for fabric and batting:

	Fabric		Batting	
Example: If you had 6 blocks in your quilt	#1 22"	#2 22"	#1 22"	#2 22"
	#3 22"	#4 22"	#3 22"	#4 22"
	#5 22"	#6 22"	#5 22"	#6 22"

Sometimes, however, material that is sold as 44" or 45" actually turns out to be 42" or 43" when it comes out of the washing machine. If this should happen to you, simply divide the width of the fabric you have in half, and use that as your size. Your block, therefore, may be 21" or 21½" rather than 22". This is okay. Simply plan on making your borders an inch or so larger than the planning diagram, and your quilt will turn out the right size. The important thing to remember, however, is to make all sides of the square the same measurement. Do not have the block be 22" on the top and bottom and 21" on the sides. **You must work with a square.** Make your block 21" on all four sides.

Step Three:
Sewing the Log Cabin Blocks

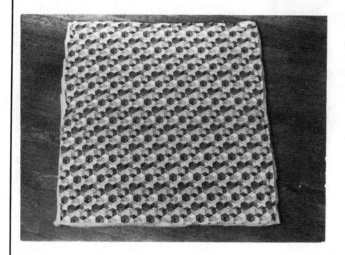

Lay one square of batting on the floor or on a table. Place one square of back fabric on top of the batt. The right side of the fabric should be facing you. Place pins in the four corners and in the middle of each length as shown.

With your machine set on the longest stitch it has, baste the two layers of back and batt together. The fabric should be on top as you sew. Use a ¼" seam allowance. If the batting should somehow seem to be a little small, just stretch it until it is the same size as the back block.

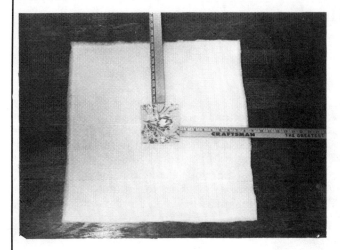

Turn the block over so the batting is facing you. Center your Center Pattern onto the block as shown. With a ruler, measure the distance from your Center Pattern to the basting stitch you have just put in. This measurement should be the same on all four sides. Write down this measurement on paper. You will need to use it in a few minutes.

When properly positioned, **lightly** pin the Center Pattern in place. Although it is important to pin lightly (so you don't gather up the material) it is also important to pin the Pattern firmly enough so it will not shift in any direction. It is best to place four pins in the Center Pattern, one along each side, as shown in this close-up.

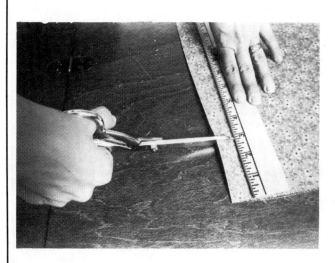

Now you must determine what width your strips will be (Fabric #1 through #8). **Take the measurement you wrote down** a few minutes ago when you centered your Center Pattern unto your block. **Divide this measurement by 4** (the number of strips you will have on each side). This will be the finished size of each strip. **To this measurement, add your seam allowance.** If you are using 5 oz. batt or less, add ½". If you are using 6 oz. or more, add ¾". As an example, if your measurement when you centered the Center Pattern was 8" on all sides, you would divide 8 by 4 and get 2. Each of your strips will finish 2". But to this 2", you must remember to add your seam allowance. If you plan on using 7.5 oz. batt, you would add ¾", so your strips would be 2¾" wide to start.

Cut or rip your strips. I prefer to rip as it is faster and usually straighter. If you bought the fabric from a store which cut it (rather than ripped it), cut a 1" notch in your fabric and rip this strip off. This will be wasted fabric but will assure you of a straight edge from which to measure. Now take your strip measurement which you have just determined and cut a notch at the correct place (as shown) and rip the fabric along its entire length. It does not matter if you rip across or down the fabric, although certain fabrics may rip easier one direction than another.

You should now iron the strips you have just ripped, since ripping often causes curled edges. It is impossible to sew an accurate ¼" seam allowance if the edges of the strip are not lying flat. Try to set up your ironing board in a convenient spot. I have mine right next to my machine and set at the same height as my table so I do not even have to stand up to iron.

Take a strip of Fabric #1 and lay it on your Center Pattern, right sides together. Start the strip where the Center Pattern starts. Do not worry if it is much longer than the Center Pattern. It should be. Do not cut it shorter, but leave it as it is.

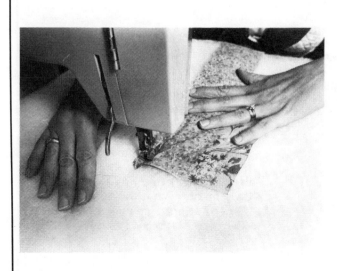

Set your machine so that it will sew 10 stitches per inch. (Most machines will easily handle this. If your machine seems to sew sluggishly or the stitches seem too small, set it for 6 or 8 stitches per inch.) Stitch the strip to the Center Pattern using a ¼" seam allowance. Backstitch or stitch in place at the start of the strip. Stitch only until you come to the end of the Center Pattern. Backstitch one or two stitches and cut your top thread. **Do not cut your bobbin thread.** You will not cut any bottom threads until the entire block is completed! Also be sure to backstitch sparingly. It is best to stitch in place if your machine has that option, since everything you do on the front shows on the back.

Lift up the remaining length of Strip #1 and cut it off even with the Center Pattern.

Open up Strip #1 so that its right side is facing you. Smooth it out with your fingers.

Turn the block in your machine 90° to your left. The strip you just sewed on should now be on top of the Center Pattern as you look at it. Now take **the same strip of Fabric #1** (you use the same material twice in a row) and place it on the Center Pattern as shown, right sides together. Start the strip even with the material of the previous strip and sew to the end of the Center Pattern. Backstitch, cut the strip off even with the edge of the Center Pattern, cut your top thread, open up the strip and smooth it out.

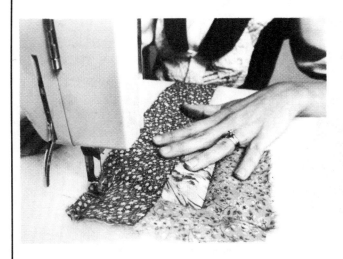

Again turning your block 90° to the left, take a strip of Fabric #2 and repeat the same steps: sew, stitch, cut the strip off even, cut the top thread, open up the strip and smooth it out. You may wonder why I continually mention such an obvious step as opening the strip and smoothing it out. I mention it because it is the mistake most often made by beginners. Sometimes people get so excited making this block, and so eager to watch it grow, that they forget to open up the previous strip before sewing on the next. Since the only remedy is to rip out the strips, believe me, no one makes this mistake twice, but I'd like to prevent you from making it even once!

Turn the block and repeat the same steps, again using Fabric #2. Sew, backstitch, cut the strip off evenly, cut the top thread, open up the strip and smooth it out.

Now take a strip of Fabric #3 and repeat the steps. Turn, sew, backstitch, cut strip and top thread, open up and smooth out strip.

Using Fabric #3 again, repeat the steps: Turn, sew, backstitch, cut strip and top thread, open up and smooth out strip.

Sew on Fabrics #4, #5, #6, #7, and #8 in a similar manner. Remember to use each fabric twice in a row. (Picture shows Fabric #7 being sewn.)

Your block should now look like this.

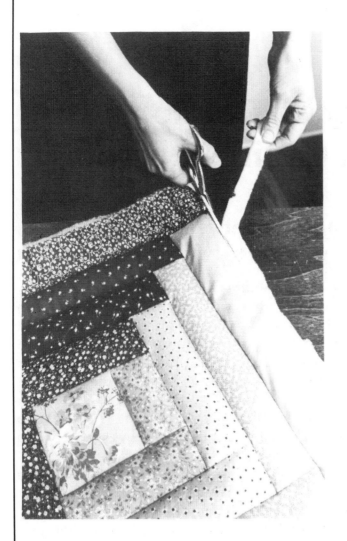

Trim off any excess batting from edges of block. Turn the block over and cut off all loose bobbin threads.

Your block is now finished. Sew all the other blocks in your quilt in the same fashion. I've found the following preparations help the sewing go faster. I sew all my Center Patterns first. Then I sew all my back fabrics to my batting blocks at one time. I tear all my strips at one time, iron them, and hang each different fabric on a separate wire clothes hanger. (After making one block, you'll be able to estimate how many additional strips of each fabric you will need. Don't rip any more strips than you think are necessary. You'll want to save any excess yardage for other sewing projects.) I keep the wire hangers hanging from the ironing board in my sewing room. I take a strip off as I need it and when I'm done sewing for the day, I simply put the hangers in the closet. This keeps my sewing room looking neat.

Chapter 3

Joining the Blocks: Diamond Strip Quilts and Log Cabin Quilts

Joining Blocks Without Borders Between the Blocks

After making all the blocks in your quilt, lay them out on the floor and see which blocks fit together best along side each other. Sometimes if you turn a block upside down it will fit better against another. This is especially important in the Diamond Strip quilt in which each strip meets another. In the Log Cabin quilt you can arrange the blocks all sorts of ways to get different patterns; such as "Barn Raising" or "Straight Furrow" for example. Experiment and see which design is most appealing to you. If one or two squares seem to be a bit smaller or larger than others, put them in the corners where only two sides of them will join up with other blocks.

Once you have the blocks laid out in the way you wish, find some way to number them so you'll always know where they go. One effective method is to put 1 pin in the center of Block #1, 2 pins in the center of Block #2, and so forth. Another numbering method is to put pieces of masking tape on each block with its number written on it. Numbering the blocks allows you to pick them up and toss them on the bed or on a table without losing their order.

To join the blocks together, start with Blocks #1 and #2. Turn them right sides together and pin through the blocks (pin through all layers). It is important to pin often — every two inches or so. Pinning often makes the blocks flatter and easier to fit under the sewing machine. If you are making the Diamond Strip quilt, place a pin in each seam in the top block, matching it with the corresponding seam in the bottom block.

After you have pinned the two blocks together, open them up. Check to see how well the seams join together. If the seams do not meet properly, try repinning. If you see tucks or folds in one block, try pulling the tucked material firmly into the seam allowance, and see if the tuck won't disappear.

When you are satisfied with your pinning job, you are ready to sew. If you are making the Diamond Strip quilt, use a ½" seam allowance when joining the blocks. This extra roomy seam allowance makes the blocks easier to sew and match properly. When sewing the Log Cabin blocks together, however, you must use a ¼" seam allowance. Any larger allowance would cut into the pattern of the blocks and thus destroy the unity of the arrangement.

Your first step is to machine baste along the edges of the blocks you have pinned together. Use the longest machine stitch you have. If you are using the large corsage pins, be sure to remove them as you sew. Otherwise, you may break quite a few machine needles!

After machine basting the two blocks together, open them up. Check that seams still match properly (they could have slipped during the sewing). Also check for tucks on the top side of your quilt. If you have either problem, see if you can correct it by simply ripping out an inch or so of your basting stitches. Adjust your fabric and resew and see if your results aren't better.

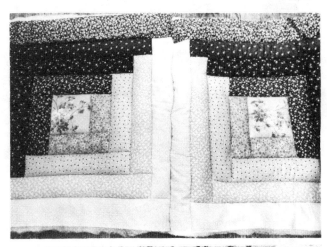

Log Cabin Quilt Blocks incorrectly pinned together.

Diamond Strip Quilt Blocks incorrectly pinned together.

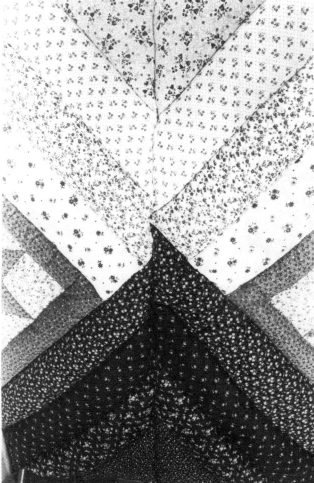

Log Cabin Quilt Blocks correctly pinned together.

Diamond Strip Quilt Blocks correctly pinned together.

Assuming you are now satisfied with the result, sew twice more along the same seam line with what I call a "real stitch" (10 to 12 stitches per inch). This may seem like a lot of sewing to you — once basted and twice with a real stitch — but it only takes a few minutes and it's definitely worth it. The most vulnerable part of the quilt is where the blocks are joined, and you certainly wouldn't want your quilt to fall apart after all the work you've put into it!

When joining the blocks together, you want to work with small units as long as possible. The best way is to sew rows of blocks going across the quilt, and then join the rows. The following charts illustrate this principle. They suggest the order in which blocks should be sewn for two different size quilts.

9 Block Quilt

#1	#2	#3
#4	#5	#6
#7	#8	#9

1. Sew #1 to #2
2. Sew #1/2 to #3
3. Sew #4 to #5
4. Sew #4/5 to #6
5. Sew #7 to #8
6. Sew #7/8 to #9
7. Sew #1/2/3 to #4/5/6
8. Sew #1/2/3/4/5/6 to #7/8/9

16 Block Quilt

#1	#2	#3	#4
#5	#6	#7	#8
#9	#10	#11	#12
#13	#14	#15	#16

1. Sew #1 to #2
2. Sew #3 to #4
3. Sew #1/2 to #3/4
4. Sew #5 to #6
5. Sew #7 to #8
6. Sew #5/6 to #7/8
7. Sew #9 to #10
8. Sew #11 to #12
9. Sew #9/10 to #11/12
10. Sew #13 to #14
11. Sew #15 to #16
12. Sew #13/14 to #15/16
13. Sew #1/2/3/4 to #5/6/7/8
14. Sew #9/10/11/12 to #13/14/15/16
15. Sew #1/2/3/4/5/6/7/8 to
    #9/10/11/12/13/14/15/16.

After all the blocks in your quilt have been joined together, lay your quilt on the floor, right side down. Your next step is to cover the seams on the back of the quilt which you have just put in. (If you are sewing a Diamond Strip quilt and have taken ½" seams, you may have quite a bit of batting showing on the back side. You may trim some of this off. Feel free to trim quite close to your seams. Remember, you have sewn the seam three times, so it is quite secure.)

You may use the same material of the back of the blocks of your quilt to cover the seams, or you may use a contrasting fabric. Using the same material will cause the seams to disappear. A contrasting fabric will set off the individual blocks and create a different effect. Either choice is pleasing, so choose the one you most prefer.

Take a long strip of the material you have selected to cover your seams. It is okay to piece this strip. The strip should be the length of your blocks joined together, plus about 5 extra inches. Make the strip approximately 3" wide. With your iron, press in a ¼" hem on each side of the strip, all the way down its length. Now take this strip and place it on the back of your quilt, centering it atop the seam you wish to cover. Lightly pin the strip in place.

You must now hand stitch this strip onto your quilt. If you machine stitched the strip atop the back, the stitches would show on the front of your quilt, and you don't want that. The stitch I use to cover my seams is called the blind stitch; it is also called a hemming stitch. It is extremely strong, and practically invisible when properly done.

Start with the same color thread you have been using for the back of your quilt. Thread your needle, double your thread to a distance of about 12"-15" and tie a knot at the end.

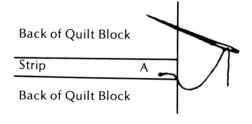

Begin with your needle in the strip. Come through Point A. Point A should be very close to the edge of the strip.

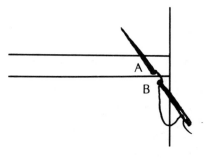

Put needle through Point B and return underneath strip through Point A again.

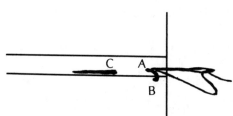

Put needle back through Point A once more and go underneath the strip approximately ½" to Point C. Come up through Point C.

This is one completed stitch. Point C would now become Point A and you would begin again. Once you get the knack of this stitch, it goes very quickly, although the first ones you do may feel awkward. I keep the quilt in my lap while I hand sew, although you could put it on a table if it felt more comfortable to you.

Generally, I sew down one side of the strip for as long as one length of a threaded needle will take me. Then I sew another length of thread on the other side of the strip directly opposite the first. I continue down until the entire strip is sewn on. If there is any extra length of stripping left, cut it off. Sew all strips in one direction first, then sew all strips in the other direction. When crossing seams, simply sew the second strip atop the first.

You are now ready to put the final borders around your quilt. Turn to Chapter 4 of this book entitled, "Finishing The Quilt — Outside Borders."

Summary of Steps in "Joining Blocks Without Borders"

1. Arrange blocks on floor in way they best fit next to each other.
2. Number the blocks.
3. Join Block #1 to Block #2
   A. Pin right sides together
   B. Check if seams match
      1. Repin if necessary
   C. Machine Baste Blocks together — 6 stitches per inch
      1. Use ½" seam allowance for Diamond Strip Quilt
      2. Use ¼" seam allowance for Log Cabin Quilt
   D. Check for tucks and to see if seams still match
      1. Rip, adjust and rebaste if necessary
   E. Sew seams twice more with "real stitch" — 10 or 12 stitches per inch.
4. Follow chart for order in joining remaining blocks together.
5. Cover seams on back of quilt.
   A. Trim off any excess batting on Diamond Strip Quilt
   B. Use strip of fabric 3" wide by the length of the quilt plus 5".
   C. Iron in hem along lengths of strip.
   D. Hand sew strip in place.*

*Do you absolutely, positively hate hand sewing? There is one alternative open to you. If your machine has a blind hemming stitch on it, you can sew your strips on with this, and it generally will not show on the top of your quilt. However, it is very awkward, especially with large quilts, shoving the bulk of the quilt under the machine head. You'll have to decide which technique is easier for you. Most of my students have decided that hand sewing is the way to go.

Joining Blocks With Borders Between the Blocks

Traditionally, borders are not put between the blocks of a Log Cabin quilt. Therefore, the following directions apply to the Diamond Strip quilt.

To begin, lay out your finished blocks on the floor. See which blocks fit together best along side each other. Sometimes rearranging the blocks or turning some upside down, will give you a better fit.

Once you have the blocks laid out the way they fit best with each other, number them so you will not lose their order. Put a small piece of paper with a number written on it in the center of each square.

You are now ready to join Block #1 to Block #2. Rip a piece of top border material that is the length of your block plus 1", and whose width is the finished size of the border (as shown on the planning chart) plus 1".

Let's use the double bed bedspread, 94" x 94" as an example.

	4"			
#1 26"	4"	#2 26"	4"	#3 26"
		4"		
#4 26"	4"	#5 26"	4"	#6 26"
		4"		
#7 26"	4"	#8 26"	4"	#9 26"
		4"		

Our finished block size in this quilt is 26" and our finished borders are all 4". At this point in our construction of the quilt, however, each block should measure 27" square. (Remember, we started out with a 28" square of back material and batting. The quilting should have caused approximately 1" shrinkage by this stage.)

Therefore, we would cut (or rip) from our top border material a strip which is 28" long (27" + 1") and 5" wide (4" + 1"). We would cut (or rip) from our back border material another strip the same size, 28" x 5". And we would cut a strip from our batting the same size, 28" x 5".

Lay Block #1 on a firm surface, such as a table or the floor, right side facing up. On the side of Block #1 which will connect to Block #2, we will place the strips of borders and bat we just cut.

On top of Block #1, right sides together, place the strip of top border fabric. On top of the top border fabric, place the strip of batting. On the underneath side of the block, place the back border fabric, right sides together. Now pin all these layers together. Be sure to pin from the bottom (start the pins underneath the block, beginning in the back border fabric, coming through to the top strip of batting and going back through all layers to end underneath in the back border fabric). Pin quite often, every two inches or so.

Set your sewing machine on its longest basting stitch. Turn the block upside down so that the wrong side of the block is facing you, and so that the batting is on the bottom. This way the batting will not get caught in the presser foot and the pins will be easy to remove as you sew. Baste through all layers, using a ½" seam allowance.

After basting, open up the block and border, and thoroughly check them. Look for tucks and folds in the fabric. Also look to see if all layers have been caught. Sometimes the top border might be caught, but the bottom border missed during the basting. The best way to check for this is to run your finger down the seams. Open them up and see if you can see both sides — the border and the block. Do this for both the top border and the back border. If you find any errors — tucks, folds or missed sewing — now is the time to adjust and correct them. Rip out a few of the machine basting stitches, and pull the fabric together properly. Rebaste, open up, and check once more to see if it turned out right this time.

This checking may seem like a lot of work, but it takes more time to read about it than to do it, and it's well worth the trouble. Mistakes are easily corrected at this stage in the quilt, and it is important to turn out a quilt you can be proud of, and one which will hold together through the years.

Assuming now that your checking process has turned up nothing wrong, the next step is to sew down the basting line with a "real stitch" — 10 or 12 stitches per inch. Your machine should be able to handle this easily, the basting stitch has flattened down the material enough so that it will easily go under the presser foot. I sew two seams with the "real stitch," so altogether the borders are sewn on three times — once basted and twice real. This may seem like a lot of sewing to you, but quilts are most vulnerable where blocks are joined together, and this extra sewing makes them extremely durable and hardy.

Now pick up Block #2. Place it next to Block #1. Take the top border (only the top border) from Block #1 and pin it to Block #2, right sides together. Open up the blocks now and check to see if the strips in the block are matching up. You want the strips in the blocks to look like they would match up if they were meeting each other directly. If yours don't, repin. Once you are satisfied with the pinning, machine baste the top border to Block #2. Open it up again, and recheck to see if the blocks still line up. If they do, you are ready to sew down the basting line twice more with a "real stitch." This time, however, catch the batting as you sew the top border and the second block together.

Open up the blocks. On the right side, the blocks have been joined with a border which is machine sewn on both sides. This looks very nice. Now flip it over. The back side has a border machine sewn onto one block but not the other. The other side of the border is hanging loose. Fold under the loose side of the border approximately ½", and then pin this side to Block #2. This side must now be hand stitched down. You can use the blind stitch as illustrated in the preceding pages (see Joining Blocks Without Borders Between the Blocks).

You are now ready to join the remaining blocks. The procedure is the same. The following charts will give you the order in which blocks should be joined. The point to remember is that you want to work with small units as long as possible. Therefore, the best way is to join rows of blocks, and then to join the rows together. The numbers in circles in the charts below show the order in which the borders are sewn on between the blocks.

6 Block Quilt

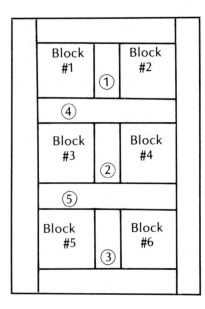

9 Block Quilt

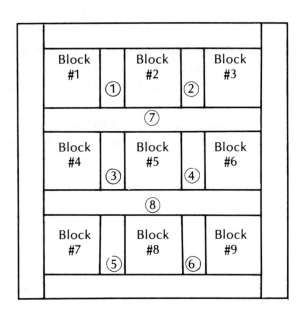

Summary of Steps in "Joining Blocks With Borders"

1. Arrange blocks on floor in way they best fit next to each other.
2. Number the blocks
3. Prepare border materials
   - A. Cut border fabrics (for top and back side of quilt) 1" longer than block length and 1" wider than finished width of border.
   - B. Batting is always cut the same size as the border fabrics
4. Join Blocks together
   - A. Block #1
     1. Place Block #1 on floor or table so that top side of block is facing you
     2. Place top border on top of block — rights sides together
     3. Place back border on back of block — right sides together
     3. Place batting on top of top border
     4. Pin all layers together.
     5. Turn block upside down and machine baste layers together using a ½" seam allowance.
     6. Open up and examine blocks and borders — check that you have caught all fabrics in all places, also check for tucks
        - a. Adjust if necessary
        - b. Re-baste
        - c. Check again
     7. Sew seams with "real stitch" (10-12 stitches per inch) twice.
   - B. Block #2
     1. Take top border fabric only, and pin to top side of Block #2 — right sides together
     2. Open up the blocks — check to see if strips of two blocks match up
        - a. Adjust if necessary
     3. Machine baste top border to Block #2 using ½" seam allowance
     4. Open up and examine blocks and borders — check that you have caught all fabrics in all places, also check for tucks
        - a. Adjust if necessary
        - b. Re-baste
        - c. Check again
     5. Sew seam twice more with a "real stitch," these two times catching the batting as well as the top border
     6. Turn Blocks over. Hand stitch loose side of back border to Back side of Block #2
5. Follow charts for order in joining remaining blocks together.

Chapter 4
Finishing the Quilt

Outside Borders

At this point all your blocks have been made and joined together. Take a yardstick or tape measure and measure your quilt. See what size it is now. Add on to this the finished size of the outside borders you plan to sew on. Will your quilt turn out the right size? Will it be large enough? Will it be too big? Now is the time to make any adjustments necessary. You can make the borders larger or smaller than were previously planned. You can add on additional borders around the outside of the quilt, or eliminate ones if you need. The only rules I follow are these: never make a border less than 2" wide (too much trouble for the result) and never make a border wider than 6" (too much batting which isn't fastened down — I prefer a 3" and a 4" border to one 7" border). Remember also that borders do not have to be the same size all the way around. It is acceptable to have a 6" border on the top and bottom of the quilt, and 3" borders on the sides. It also looks fine to have two borders on the top and bottom of your quilt, and only one on the sides, if you wish a rectangular quilt.

The directions which follow are for a quilt with two outside borders. If your quilt has only one outside border, skip ahead a few paragraphs to "Final Borders." If you quilt has more than two borders, simply repeat the steps for the first border until you come to the final border.

The First Outside Border

You will need a long border piece for the top of your quilt, another for the back side of your quilt, and a strip of batting. All three of these should be the same size. The strips of borders and batt should be the length of your quilt in its present stage (Blocks sewn together) plus 2". The extra 2" is for insurance, you may not need it. However, nothing is more frustrating than finding out you need less than ½" extra in the length of the border you cut, so I always allow an extra 2" for variances in measuring. The width of the strips should be the finished size of the border plus 1" for seam allowances if it is the Diamond Strip Quilt or ¾" seam allowance if it is a Log Cabin Quilt. Don't worry if you do not have a piece of material that is 90" or more, depending on what you need. It is perfectly acceptable to piece material together until it is the proper length. You may also piece batting if necessary. Simply butt the ends of the batting up next to each other (do not overlap) and baste them together by hand.

Lay your quilt on the floor, right side facing up. Lay the top border strip along the top side of the quilt, right sides together. Lay the batting strip on top of this. On the back side of the quilt lay the back border, right sides together. Pin the layers together, pinning quite often, about every 2". Machine baste these layers together, setting your machine on the longest stitch it has. Use a ½" seam allowance for the Diamond Strip Quilt and a ¼" seam allowance for the Log Cabin Quilt. After basting, open up the border and check it. Look for folds and tucks. Also check that both borders caught the block. The best way to check is to run your fingers down the seam.

Can you see both the border and the block? If not, rip out a few stitches, pull the layers together, and resew. If everything is satisfactory, sew down the basting seam twice more with a "real stitch" (10-12 stitches per inch).

Your first border is now done. If there is any excess length of border and batt, cut it off even with the edge of the quilt. (Remember our extra 2" for insurance — maybe you didn't need it.) Repeat the same process for your next border on the side directly opposite the one you started with. Then put borders on the remaining two sides of your quilt, if your planning chart calls for them. These borders will be cut longer than the first two you sewed on. They should be cut the length of your blocks sewn together, plus the width of the two borders you just attached, plus the extra 2" for insurance. The method of sewing them on is the same as before.

This next step is an optional one. It takes about an hour of your time, but I feel it's worth the trouble. At this point all your borders are flopping around. Take the borders on the top of your quilt and smooth them out. Pin the top border fabric, the batting, and the back border fabric together along the unsewn long edge. Machine baste, using a ¼" seam allowance, these three layers together. You now have an easy unit to which you will attach your next border. Repeat this step on the remaining borders.

Final Outside Border:

The final border is put on the same way as the first outside border with one important exception: the back border fabric is cut 2" wider than the front border fabric.* Therefore, if your final outside border is to be a finished width of 4", you would cut the front border 5" wide and the back border 7" wide. The batting would be cut 5" wide, the size of the skinnier border.

Following the directions under First Outside Borders, sew the final border on the top of your quilt. Use a ½" seam allowance. (The only exception to this will be if you are only putting one border around a Log Cabin Quilt. Then this border will need a ¼" seam allowance rather than a ½". However, if you have already sewn one border around a Log Cabin Quilt, you should use a ½" seam allowance in all succeeding borders.) Sew your next final border strip on the bottom of the quilt, directly opposite the side you just finished.

Before sewing on the remaining side final borders, lay your quilt out on the floor. Spread the top and bottom back borders out. Notice how they extend further than the top border and the batting? When you pin on the remaining two side borders, start the top fabric even with the edge of the top border fabric you just attached, start the batting even with the batting, and the back border fabric even with the edge of the back border. End them in the same fashion: front borders even, batting even, and back borders even. Machine baste, check, and sew with a "real stitch" just as you did before.

Once more, spread out your quilt on the floor. Smooth the final borders out on all four sides. Notice how the back borders extend out about 2". All you have to do now is fold the edge of the back border under approximately ½" and then fold it over another ½" onto the top of the quilt. Pin securely along the entire edge of the folded over border. When you get to a corner of the quilt, simply shove any excess border material into the inside of the quilt. It will never show on the outside, and the extra bulk makes the corners firm. You may turn either a square corner or a mitered one, whichever is easier for you.

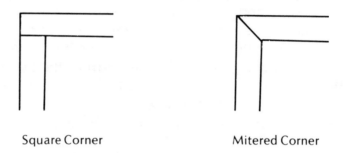

Square Corner   Mitered Corner

Now stitch the turned over back border to the top of your quilt. I machine stitch through all the layers. This holds the batting in place for the life of the quilt, so I prefer machine stitching to hand stitching. If your machine has fancy stitches, here is a good place to try one. A running zigzag stitch is a particularly pretty and easy one to sew. Stitch around all four sides of the quilt.

*The directions in the Final Outside Border assume you will want to bring the back border material over to the top side of your quilt. If the back fabric would not be attractive on the top side of your quilt, you should turn the top border fabric over to the back. Simply cut the top border 2" wider than the back. So, if your finished border width is 4", you would cut the top border 7", the back border 5" and the batting 5". Sewing instructions would be the same.

Order in which Outside Borders should be sewn onto Quilts

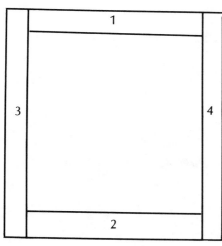

One border around quilt

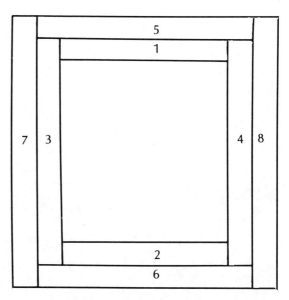

Two Borders around quilt

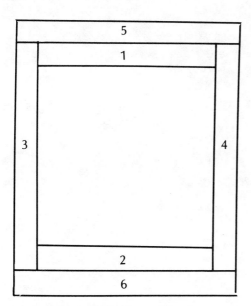

Two borders on top and bottom
One border on sides

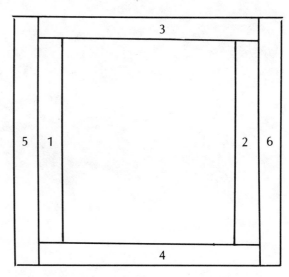

Two borders on sides
One border on top and bottom

Your quilt is now finished! Check it over to make sure there are no loose threads hanging anywhere and then go show it off. Be proud of your quilt and of yourself. You've created a work of beauty and love.

Back Cover
Top Row

(Left) Log Cabin blocks of rose and cream colored fabrics have been arranged to form a star pattern on this quilt. 100" x 100". Made by Rita Davis.

(Right) This Log Cabin Quilt has used the "Barn Raising" arrangement, creating a striking display of its blue and green blocks. 80" x 80". Made by Corliss Marsh.

Middle Row

"Evening Star" has been used as the Center Pattern in this Diamond Strip Quilt, with Borders between the Blocks. 96" x 96". Made by Rita Davis.

Bottom Row

(Left) Close up photograph of one block in Christie Chase's Diamond Strip Quilt.

(Right) Christie Chase sewed Template "D" from the "Square in a Square" Center Pattern to friendship blocks given her by members of her craft group, and used these as the Center Patterns for a delightful Diamond Strip Quilt. 84" x 84".

Quilts on the Opposite Page
Top Row

(Left) "Weathervane" has been used as the Center Pattern in this beautiful Diamond Strip Quilt fit for a twin bed. Note that the same fabrics have been used in the same order on all four sides of the Center Pattern. Made by Linda Franklin.

(Center) Blocks were joined in the "Traditional" pattern in this cozy Log Cabin Quilt made by Linda Franklin. 80" x 100".

(Right) "Square in a Square" Center Patterns have been used in this Diamond Strip twin bed quilt. 65" x 92". Owned by Catherine Davis, made by Rita Davis.

Middle Row

(Left) Red and White Log Cabin blocks make a dazzling arrangement in a pattern called "Sunshine and Shadow." 80" x 85". Made by Meg Cummins.

(Right) This attractive wallhanging is composed of four Diamond Strip Quilt Blocks, joined without borders between the blocks. "Evening Star" was used as the Center Pattern in each block. Made by Christie Chase.

Bottom Row

(Left) Log Cabin blocks of browns and blues are arranged in the "Barn Raising" pattern in this quilt owned by Ken Davis. 80" x 80". Made by Rita Davis.

(Right) This Christmas Log Cabin Quilt has red and yellow strips on one side of the block, and green strips on the other side. The blocks are set in the "Sunshine and Shadow" pattern. 100" x 100". Made by Rita Davis.

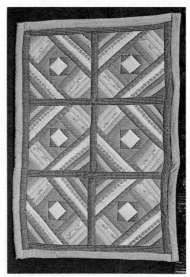